Making the Beds for the Dead

GILLIAN CLARKE was born in Cardiff in 1937, and now lives in Ceredigion. A poet, writer, playwright and tutor on the M.Phil in Creative Writing at the University of Glamorgan, she is also president of Ty Newydd, the writers' centre in North Wales which she co-founded in 1990. Carcanet publish her *Collected Poems* and *Selected Poems*.

GILLIAN CLARKE

Making the Beds for the Dead

CARCANET

Acknowledgements

Acknowledgements are due to the following where some of these poems, or versions of them, first appeared: *The New Welsh Review*; *Planet*; *PN Review*; *North*; *Wading through Deep Water: Parkinson's Disease Charity Anthology*, edited by Tony Curtis (Edge Press, 2001); BBC Radio 4; to Andrew Sclater for commissioning poems for *Bioverse: Poems for the National Botanic Garden of Wales* (HarperCollins, 2000), from which the first seedlings of 'The Stone Poems', 'The Middleton Poems' and 'The Physicians of Myddfai' have grown; to William Wilkins and Aberglasne for commissioning 'Nine Green Gardens' (Gomer Press, 2000); Colman Getty; *The Epic Poise: A Celebration of Ted Hughes*, edited by Nick Gamage (Faber, 1999); *The Way You Say the World: A Celebration for Anne Stevenson*, edited by John Lucas and Matt Simpson (Shoestring Press, 2003); the Hay Festival of Literature; *Poetry Proms*, BBC Radio 3.

Special thanks are due to the Arts Council of Wales for the Creative Wales Award which helped me to write this book.

First published in Great Britain in 2004 by
Carcanet Press Limited
Alliance House
Cross Street
Manchester M2 7AQ

A CIP catalogue record for this book is available from the British Library
ISBN 1 85754 737 3

The publisher acknowledges financial assistance from
Arts Council England

Typeset in Monotype Bembo by XL Publishing Services, Tiverton
Printed and bound in England by SRP Ltd, Exeter

Contents

For Catrin, Owain and Dylan,
a Dafydd, fel arfer

In the Beginning

'on her 7th birthday'

Holy Bible – the King James version,
soft black leather cover,
tissue pages edged in gold.
I loved the maps, the names: Jerusalem.
Askelon. The Wilderness of Shur.

And the old photographs:
caught by a camera in black and white,
women drawing water at a well,
a fisherman on the Sea of Galilee
blurred people scything corn,
mountains sharp, stone still forever.

I see it all in colour, a girl my age
two thousand years ago, or sixty years,
or now in a desert land at war, squatting
among the sheaves, arms raised,
threshing grain with a flail.

Threshing with a flail. That's it. Words
from another language, a narrative of spells
in difficult columns on those moth-thin pages,
words to thrill the heart with a strange music,
words like flail, and wilderness,
and in the beginning.

A Woman Sleeping at a Table

by Vermeer

1657. The house in Delft.
Windfalls in a bowl.
See her wake, take
an apple in one hand,
a knife in the other.

The apple has fallen
from the tree in Eden.
They are mapping the round earth,
discovering geography, astronomy,
She holds the world in her hand.

The apple turns
under the fixed stars.
Her knife cuts into the Pole
and peels the fruit in a single
ringlet of skin.

Undressed to its equator
it is half moonlight.
Then all white, naked, whole,
she slices to the star-heart
for the four quarters of the moon.

Mother Tongue

You'd hardly call it a nest,
just a scrape in the stones,
but she's all of a dither
warning the wind and sky
with her desperate cries.

If we walk away
she'll come home quiet
to the warm brown pebble
with its cargo of blood and hunger,
where the future believes in itself,

and the beat of the sea
is the pulse of a blind
helmeted embryo afloat
in the twilight of the egg,
learning the language.

The Poet's Ear

for Anne Stevenson

Nothing to do
with the clamorous city,
shouting *sotto voce* to no one
in pubs, parties, shops,
and all of us pretending to hear.

Nothing to do
with the train drumming the viaduct,
traffic tuning up at the junction,
the black stone cathedral's bells
in the frozen air.

Not wind in the feathering rusts
of the motorway angel
singing a note too high to hear,
its rasp of red dust
in the slipstream of lorries.

Nor the small talk of ewe and lamb,
or the call of the kite and the crow
over Pwll-y-March
where high notes are first to go
in the labyrinth's silence.

It is footfall. Breath. The heart
listening for the line's perfect pitch.
It's not Bach, not Schumann,
but the mind's 'cello sounding
the depths of the page.

The Fisherman

for Ted Hughes

From his pool of light in the crowded room, alone,
the poet reads to us. The sun slinks off
over darkening fields, and the moon is a stone
rolled and tumbled in the river's grief.

In a revolving stillness at the edge
of turbulent waters, the salmon hangs its ghost
in amber. On the shore of the white page
the fisherman waits. His line is cast.

The house is quiet. Under its thatch
it is used to listening. It's all ears
for the singing line out-reeled from his touch
till the word rises with its fin of fire.

The tremor in the voice betrays a hand
held tense above the surface of that river,
patient at the deep waters of the mind
for a haul of dangerous silver,

till electricity's earthed, and hand on heart
the line that arcs from air to shore is art.

The Piano

The last bus sighs through the stops of the sleeping suburb
and he's home again with a click of keys, a step on the stairs.
I see him again, shut in the upstairs sitting-room
in that huge Oxfam overcoat, one hand shuffling
through the music, the other lifting the black wing.

My light's out in the room he was born in. In the hall
the clock clears its throat and counts twelve hours
into space. His scales rise, falter and fall back –
not easy to fly on one wing, even for him
with those two extra digits he was born with.

I should have known there'd be music as he flew, singing,
and the midwife cried out, 'Magic fingers!' A small variation,
born with more, like obsession. They soon fell,
tied like the cord, leaving a small scar fading
on each hand like a memory of flight.

Midnight arpeggios, Bartok, Schubert. I remember,
kept in after school, the lonely sound of a piano lesson
through an open window between-times, sun on the lawn
and everyone gone, the piece played over and over
to the metronome of tennis. Sometimes in the small hours,

after two, the hour of his birth, I lose myself listening
to that little piece by Schubert, perfected in the darkness
of space where the stars are so bright they cast shadows,
and I wait for that waterfall of notes, as if
two hands were not enough.

Erik Satie and the Blackbird

*on listening to Satie's 'Vexations' played from noon to dawn by a relay of pianists
in Salem Chapel, Hay-on-Wye*

The blackbird sings
for eighteen hours
with a bead of rain
in its throat.
First notes at first light.
Four in the morning
and he'll be there
with his mouth full of gold.

The piano crosses an ocean
on one wing,
noon to midnight
and through to dawn.
This is the nightshift.
you and the rain
and the pianist awake,
navigating the small hours.

While the blackbird sleeps
under a dark wing,
the town breathing,
the wash of a car on a wet street,
the world turns over
in the dark. The sleepless
travel on. They know by heart
their own refrains.

The pianist doesn't turn the page.
Just back to the top
where music collects
opening its throat to the rain,
and somewhere two bells
count down the hours
towards first light, landfall,
the downpour of a blackbird singing.

The Flood Diary

The weather girl reciting river names:
Severn, Wye, Humber, Aire and Ouse.
Atlantic lows lap at our living rooms,
the familiar map stormed by electric blues.
Out there where it's real the land is sodden,
the reservoir rocks at the lip of the dam.
Beasts stand as if stillness might rescue them,
islands of rooted cattle, ewes with their lambs.
We saw it coming – months of rain, and every
river taking to the road, the Severn
swollen on its way to Shrewsbury,
a ribbon of mountain water turned
to a six-lane torrent falling a thousand feet
with boulders, mud and branches in its throat.

We borrowed a van, and took the risk,
drove ninety miles through wind and rain north-east
to a timber yard in the hills for an oak truss,
by-passed the flooded Dyfi by forest track
and mountain pass. Strapped in, transaction over,
homebound in arrowing rain, we came upon
an old man knee-deep in a broken river
his car stalled in the current, its door held open
for the river to step in. We left it locked,
drove him to a neighbouring farm, shocked
but safe, and fled before the flood engulfed us too,
thought all the perilous way of its lights warning
till the battery ran out, or the river bore it away,
my hand on your thigh in silence, the barometer falling.

*

In a house in a southern English town
beside a modest river
used to collecting the slow
chalk Downland waters,

a grand piano paddles,
wades, treads water,
is lifted, riding the flood
in the room's harbour,

becomes an ark of rosewood
engulfed in filth, in the backwash
rainbows of petrol, diesel, drains,
its music under its wing.

A wave lifts the lid
on a gleam of ivory,
Its golden name wavers
underwater and is gone,

Bechstein,
an eel of light before
centuries of music drown
and the lights go out.

★

All winter, travelling by train,
the sodden length and breadth,
I ride above floodfields.
They built the lines high,
bridging hills and hollows
with embankments and viaducts.

Station after station
platforms flash with puddles.
A city gleams across the broken waters.
A cathedral grows reflective.
Horizons drown the sun,
its colours bleeding.

In the hotel, windows weep
and television brims.
I watch the news.
A city holds its breath
above the meniscus of a river
swollen with Pennine headwaters
and rising. They'll watch all night.

★

When the rains stop
and rivers empty into the sea,

19

there will be cities whose foothold
is dislodged a little,

fields that remember
becoming the sky,

the skull of a sheep filling
with tormentil and harebells,

and somewhere, among birdsong,
woodnotes and the strings of the wind,

the carcass and white teeth
of a piano.

RS

for the poet R.S. Thomas, 1913–2000

His death
on the midnight news.
Suddenly colder.

Gold September's driven off
by something afoot
in the south-west approaches.

God's breathing in space out there
misting the heave of the seas
dark and empty tonight,

except for the one frail coracle
borne out to sea,
burning.

The Painter

for Mary Lloyd-Jones

She dips her brush in sky,
in rain, in story
and comes up with who we are.
The brush unloads its cloud in a jar
to take its place with stratocumulus,
a trace of rose in cirrus,
a thunderhead on the mountain
before precipitation.

She paints with slabs of light,
all the colours of white,
the paint tubes' poetry,
rose madder, purple madder,
ochre, umber, cerulean blue.

Even white is a prism.
Even black is reached
through the rainbow's narrowing tunnel.

★

A Stone Age hand in blood on a wall
gestures with cave beasts, script and symbol,
and the woman sign, the vulva's triangle,
the cup of pearly seed.

Print of hoof, foot, hand, paw,
clawed, cloven, chiselled, calcified.
You can hear breath and heartbeat
of a man, a beast, a woman

calling from so long ago
you can believe she stood by tallow light
to make her mark here on the page,
dipping her hand in blood.

The Stone Poems

Rock

In the subdivisions of geological time
Earth story's chaptered with eras,
paragraphed with epochs, ages, chrons,
sedimentary time laid down and shaped
with the patience of stone, silt on silt,
microbe, algae, trilobite, brachiopod,
first jellyfish, first worm,
leaf-mould, bone on bone.
Then the long upheavals, continents
lapping like plates of a baby's skull.

Hay

Speaking of stone on a day like this,
the silence, the heat, the hay-days,
when the slates creak in the sun,
the flags are too hot for the dog
and the field's dried to a thin song
of seeds and grasshoppers,
yellow rattle, harebells, the litany of grass,

any moment now there'll be the growl
of a neighbour's tractor on the lane,
then the swishing scissors of the mowing machine,
and every last grass and fallen flower of the field
by nightfall cooling under the moon
is dependent on neighbourhood
and the nourishment of rock.

Granite

PRE–CAMBRIAN

Vertiginous numbers:
seven-hundred million years,
granite from Pembrokeshire. Is it this
we tread on, this starry pavement,
the Milky Way underfoot?

Go sandalled over pavements set with granite
in a southern city of squares and geraniums,
alleyways cats-cradled with ellipses,
laundry blown in a warm wind
and bed linen laid to air over granite sills.

Sit at a cafe table in the dusk,
a glass of wine, a floor hewn from the batholith.
Take a loosened piece in your hand,
a paving sett to turn under the light
so small and heavy it can teach you gravity.

Slate

CAMBRIAN

It arrived from Gwynedd, Penrhyn slate
palletted, piled on the drive,
settled from silts and mudstones
five hundred and twenty million years ago,
bruised purple by so much time,
a history book, its pages open
for the text of lichens and weather.

It roofed Europe, made floors so cold
the rheum seeped through their bones.
Hearthstone. Threshold. Gate-post.
Dairy slabs where cream was rising gold,
and butter came in the churn, patted and ridged
with a wooden spade carved with a sheaf of wheat,
salt-butter left on a slate to bead
between the bivalves of two plates.

Like this old house between the saucers
of floor and roof, a pigeon's throat
of lapping purples, lilacs, greys,
feathering our nest under the stars.

Edward Llwyd and the Trilobite
ORDOVICIAN

Edward Llwyd, he was the curious one,
the Snowdon Lily already to his name,
nose down among the very stones of the earth,
noting 'divers flatfish' in the rocks.

Llandeilo, sixteen-ninety-nine. Forget
all that we know. Un-name the stones, the fossils,
untell the age of the Ordovician.
Count biblical time from the seventh day.

Their world was created in four-thousand-and-four BC,
and the stone fish he netted from Carmarthen silts
were 'figured stones' placed there by God, creation's
little finishing touches, like the stars in heaven.

A strike of his hammer broke the heart of limestone
clean as a conker, and a trilobite stared
with four-hundred and sixty-five-million-year-old eyes
from a dark age deeper than his fathoming.

Landfall
SILURIAN

Wake in a blaze of moonlight.
Sit up too quickly. Dizzy. Don't
be surprised to find yourself in the Silurian,
your house in deep water.

On the map of the past
this place was far out at sea,
old Ceredigion not born
from the Iapetus Ocean.

Land out of its depth, finding fall
from Aberystwyth grits and mudstones,
storm-driven sands out of waters
too old and too deep for life.

So your bed's on the tilt and spinning,
walls cart-wheeling on four corners,
then the oak chest slides, sucked down
the turbidity currents of sleep.

Your body knows this.
Walk the cliffs. Look down
to a tumble of choughs, and farther, below,
a sea-locked cove of ochre sand you yearn for.

Feel vertigo's pendulum pull at your heart,
and underground, underfoot,
the powerful surge of the Iapetus Ocean
dragging its tether.

Woman Washing her Hair
DEVONIAN
for David

A block of yellow sandstone in the sun.
You tap and chisel in the open air
until you find her in the coarse-grain stone,
a woman on her haunches, pouring her hair.

Curled, primitive, crouched on the folds
of her thighs. You comb stone into strands
furrowed like the steep fields
of Brecon's old red ploughland,

like plaiting and contending waterfalls,
sands and sediments, the dreadlocks of the sea.
Half emerged, unfinished, not quite free,
slowly the sandstone woman, leaning still

over waters that are not quite there,
crouches, washing her hair.

The Stone Hare
LOWER CARBONIFEROUS
for Meic Watts

Think of it waiting three hundred million years,
not a hare hiding in the last stand of wheat,
but a premonition of stone, a moonlit reef
where corals reached for the light through clear
waters of warm Palaeozoic seas.
In its limbs lies the story of the earth,
the living ocean, then the slow birth
of limestone from the long trajectories
of starfish, feather-stars, crinoids and crushed shells
that fill with calcite, harden, wait for the quarryman,
the timed explosion and the sculptor's hand.
Then the hare, its eye a planet, springs from the chisel
to stand in the grass, moonlight's muscle and bone,
the stems of sea lilies slowly turned to stone.

Coal
UPPER CARBONIFEROUS
for Glyndŵr Thomas, 1915–1995

From Abercarn, Gwent,
from the tropical swamp that laid down the coal
he cut when he was a boy,
fourteen years old and a real man now,
working the stint at his father's side,

Deep under the earth, labouring at the face
in lamp-swept darkness, he'd ache
at a sudden breath of bluebells brought
by a May wind in the downdraft,
for the sunlit woods he'd miss that shift.

We bring in a scuttleful, every shovel
haunted by hands, hibernating newts,
little dragons of damp places,
saved one by one from the fire,
their fingers cold on our skin.

Mesozoic

Time of the dinosaur.
First paw-print. First hoofbeat.
First mammals of swamp and shore,
first of the cold-bloods dreaming on stones.

And at its humid, balmy close,
ammonite and dinosaur dead,
rich silts flood the valleys,
and the garden begins.

The Middleton Poems

the National Botanic Garden of Wales

The Ice-House

The door leads into the hill
to a bat hibernaculum,
house of wintering shadows

folded and packed as tight as ice,
till warmth thaws them, sends them skittering
into a summer dusk.

Paxton's ice-house, not Frigidaire,
not our immaculate tabernacles
of white enamel stowed with cold.

We sip, watching the evening bats,
the tinkle in a glass reminding water
of the earth it came from.

Ice Harvest

With block and tackle, grappling iron, axe,
they'd lift the lid off the lake. In a rare year
an acre could yield a thousand tons.

Then heavy horses hauled it up the hill,
blocks of luminous blue, sky turned to glass,
each one clear to the needle of light at its core.

In a mild year they'd take ponies
to the mountain, unlock ravines of snow,
or sever the tangled locks of waterfalls.

Plumbing

A lemon bloomed with frost,
hollowed and filled with sweet snow.
A bowl of ice and Muscat grapes.
Breath on a glass of wine.

Paxton knew these things, and brought from India
his dreams of ice and water engineering,
and from the Mughal gardens his design
of cool reflections and the sound of water.

From his Tower he'd see it all: a garden of streams,
sluices, dams, cascades, and a house on a hill
in a chain of lakes, with reservoirs and ice-ponds,
the healing waters of chalybeate springs.

He piped water to his gate for public use,
to save the rural poor from filth and fevers,
a hundred years ahead of his time devised,
a water system for Carmarthen.

Cisterns, pipes, drains, faucets, closets,
water flowed through his house. Above the springs
with their medicinal powers, he built a bath-house
in a garden, that they might take the waters,

herbal aromas, minerals and steam,
bring colour back to dear Maria's cheek,
cooling the fevers as they basked
in water's opulence.

A Banquet at Middleton

What a night in the vale of Tywi. Guests
from London. Paxton's house complete, windows
flame with candlelight. Bat-shadows
scribble on the dusk, a ring of lakes
reflect the house. Music. Murmurs of silk.
They sip their wine from goblets made of ice,
admire the fountain table-centrepiece,
a swan afloat on snow and honeyed milk,

and trapped in an obelisk of glass, live fish
flickering. Piled in frozen pyramids,
ice-apples, peaches, mulberries, figs,
glowing jellies, junkets, creams, a dish
of fine rose-scented butter. Such a stir
it must have caused in deep Carmarthenshire.

The Great Glasshouse
AD 2000

The architect's vision, an inclined ellipse,
three hundred tons of steel and glass
and an ice-dome rises among the slopes
above the Tywi. From a wilderness
of weeds in the print of the lost forecourt
where Paxton's house once stood, an oval
cathedral of geometry and light
constructed out of hoops of tubular steel
and a thousand sheets of rain-washed glass.
A torus, raising its glistening shape,
like a coracle upturned in the grass
apt to the bowl of sky and hillscape,
a phial for a Mediterranean climate,
a lens to look at stars on a clear night.

The Olive Grove

From the mountains above Almuñicar,
Granada, eighteenth-century Spain,
roots bound in gesso for the journey,
ancient trees veiled in horticultural fleece,
against Atlantic westerlies.

Even here, under glass,
they are Mediterranean,
holding time in the heartwood as rock does,
their stillness animal, knuckle, elbow, wrist,
creased like human skin.

Their darkness is Cézanne's,
where rock, tree, sky, blaze
with the light and dark of sun and stone,
black branches, smoky foliage wreathed
in a grove of olives and wild flowers.

Two-hundred-year-old trees
slowly, slowly grow towards the light,
the almost midnight sunsets of midsummer,
temperate winter skies, in a little earth
between two saucers, of rock, of glass.

★

'Like gold', she used to say of the oil
in the two-ounce bottle kept in the medicine cupboard.
She'd warm the drops and let them, bead by bead,
into the sounding pain of a child's ear.
and the spell was cast.

If they could see us now as we dip our bread
in saucers of green-gold extra-virgin
bought by the litre, lick our fingers clean
then slip the fruits into our mouths,
taking the flesh till there's nothing left but the stone.

El Niño in the Walled Garden

The moon and planets step out in a row
along the moon-road. Close doors. Draw curtains now.
The wild child's fists are full of snow.

Somewhere on earth this year there are no birds,
no wing-beat in the breeding-grounds, no herds
of travelling buffalo, no words

to weigh the heaviest blizzard ever known,
the worst tornado flattening little towns,
the slash and burn that brings great forests down.

Let the skylark sing its heart out in the air.
Let the moon reflect in the wide-awake eye of the hare
alert in its form. Let the otter come home to the river.

It's time to get it right, to recreate Eden
from a wilderness in a walled garden,

safe house for barn owl and water-vole,
for Natterer's bat and pipistrelle,
for the hairy and the garlic-scented snails,

for *Punctum pygmaeum,* the size of a pinhead,
for adder and dormouse, newt and toad,

for the *derwydd* daffodil, the Snowdon lily,
for fungi, lichens, and that one rare tree,

the single remaining specimen
in a cliff face in Brecon.

The Physicians of Myddfai

Llyn-y-Fan Fach

A crack in glass,
the scream and shadow
of a Hawk, close and low
enough to blow the heart.

Like a bowl of milk
the mountain cups the lake
where the Ages of Stone,
Bronze and Iron left their bones
under the earth, under the water
with the lake king's daughter.

Look into that surface.
It's not your face
you see, but hers,
as the wind stirs
water's mirror.
Wind turns history's
pages, each leaf
not yours but a people's grief.

Legend

Every day he dreamed her face
a ferment on the surface.
With his mother's bread
he'd win her to his bed.
The spell was buttermilk and barm,
grains ground between stones,
pummelled and set to warm
by a fire or under the sun.
Such leavening as suddenly she breaks
the surface of the lake.

Three loaves,
three chances for love
to cross the boundaries
of time and history.
On the third day she was his own.
Three strikes of metal and she'd gone.

The ages drown,
dissolved into the past,
stories of the land half lost
in myths and silts
of ancient settlements.

Healers

At Myddfai now, their names
are on the gravestones,
sons of the sons of the sons
of the woman of water
and the man of the earth,
their secret buried with their bones.

Somewhere down the line
myth became history,
and slow repeating time
passed down the story
in the mother tongue
to the young.

From them we might have learned
the healing power of plants.
Will this be the day we loose
the furious gene, trampling
the heal-all that grows
in a field singing with bees,
that might have given us what science
seeks in its test-tubes and trays?

★

The wind is bitter
and the air is stone.
We throw bread on the water
for a wild swan swimming alone.

Nine Green Gardens

He has a proud hall.
A fortress made bright by whitewash
And encompassing it all around,
Nine green gardens.
        Lewys Glyn Cothi (c. 1420–1489)

The Yew Tunnel in Winter

Listen to sap rise, unstoppable flood,
for all the centuries as the tap-roots grew,
pumping through branches to the stirring bud
from deepest earth. In graveyards they say a yew
sends a root into the mouths of all the dead.
Here, sense all that power snowed in and still,
shut in the dream of winter and history
at the end of a muffled lane below Grongar Hill.
The garden's under wraps. The sorrow trees
let in, like moonlight, little webs of snow,
white footfalls through the arching clerestories.
Grown from a seed five centuries ago
from the gut of a bird, the Age of Hywel done,
the poetry of gardens yet to come.

The Parapet Walk

Rumours of religious settlements
leave silences among the cloister stones,
and underfoot, a shadow in each cowled arch.
Cron Gaer. A circle hill-fort. Roman and Celt.
The Kingdom of Hywel Dda. Even their bones
are gone, ground to a fine tilth under mulch,
leaf-mould, soils and river-silts.
Lewys Glyn Cothi's nine green gardens
folded in fields of war named bloodily
like our century's fields of guilt,
Cae Tranc, Cae Dial, Cae'r Ochain, Cadfan.
The words are blood and bone of butchery.
Whitsun, 1257, the battle of Coed Llathen,
a thousand Saxons dead, brief victory Llywelyn's.

The Cloister Garden

When he came home to Aberglasne,
crusader, troubadour, on the road from Europe,
shouldering arms, a lute, a sack of dreams,
did he, poet or soldier, bring from Italy
a vision of a garden on a slope
above a valley fed with mountain streams?
Abbot. Landowner. Who planned
this cloister garden apt to the inclination
of the hill? Who set a pavement here
for gentry to stroll on levelled land
or a ghost to go in slippered contemplation
under the ancient shadow of Cron Gaer?
Either way, it's here, the hanging garden
of another time, a rediscovered Eden.

A Sad Story

Places are made of hearsay and story.
There's talk in these trees of five young servant girls
found dead in their beds one winter morning,
choked, they say, by the fumes of a blocked chimney.
That dawn the house woke to cold ash, no curl
of smoke from thirty hearths burning.
The silence of the dead instead of chatter
and quick feet running on the stairs,
fuel for the fires and jugs of scalding water,
slop buckets, sculleries awash, clatter
of crockery on slate, the chink of silver.
People of no account, poor farmers' daughters.
No names. No documents. No graves. Instead
just talk of a tragedy, five young girls dead.

Church Wood

Beyond the wall and the ruined aviary,
a wood where trees shadow a small pool.
Outside the wire the fields are nitrogen green.
Away from the house and its raucous rookery,
the contemplation garden's quiet and cool.
We walk as if we own the place, unseen
in the privacy and silence of still water.
Somewhere, the gunfire of a wren in an ash.
To the north, the Via Julia Maritima,
now become the humming loud A40.
John Dyer's Grongar Hill lies west
beyond the garden's *terza rima*.
A poet shares a gardener's grand design:
sound, pattern, meaning, double digging, line.

The Upper Walled Garden

In the hot box of the upper walled garden
raised beds lie ready for the gardener's design,
a Celtic cross, two circles cut by paths,
a red kite's view of curve and line.
Aconitum, Alchemilla, Amaryllis, Angelica

Down here in the heat, two survivors: a fig tree
rooted in the wall, and an ancient apple leans
its weight against the earth, its hard fruit set
among the drum and dither of wild bees.
Camassia, Campanula, Clematis, Crocosmia

Once a kitchen garden, hives under apple trees,
where maids came gathering for the table.
A litany of plant names now, and earthy airs
rise from the garden's seething crucible.
Euphorbia, Rudbeckia, Iris germanica.

Listen to the garden's Latin, the *missa cantata*
of *Wisteria sinensis, Prunus lusitanica.*

The Lower Walled Garden

Past the old apple tree askew the path,
down through the door in the wall. A blackbird singing.
Young sapling trees still potted and bound.
Malus sargentii, browned in the aftermath
of a late frost. Silvers of a buzzard turning.
It could be the secret garden, the one not found,
garden beyond garden deep in the lee
of Grongar hill. From the sky you'd see a view
of four rectangles edged with box,
a tunnel of crab apple trees
and future walks in shady avenues
on crossed paths with a roundel at the crux,
and off centre, at the heart, an apple tree,
its fallen shadow old as history.

The Pool Garden

The cuckoo's late, two notes in the weeping ash.
Last call, C and A flat, before
its voice breaks and the summer's older.
The kite circles land grown lush
with sorrows of another century's war.
In garlands of builder's ribbon, gaudy
oceans of crumpled plastic, a machine
leans on its claw. The clay is caterpillar
tracked with chevrons, the water cloudy
from the digger's delicate bucket work, green
with weed and reflections. Once viticulture
flourished where the hot border's planned
on the south wall. A thrush picks the churned soil,
alone with the garden gods beside the pool.

The Stream Garden

Damp ground between the pool garden and the wood
where watercress was grown and greenhouses stood,
where a CAT track machine rests on its shovel
like a horse asleep, with loosestrife, tormentil,
wild rhubarb, huge umbellifers,
and held by its neighbours, one fallen conifer.
Think of it creaking in wind, the wrench of its fall
through fists of giant hogweed, and all
the sharp, musk-loaded, insect-shining scent
of earth and air disturbance as it went
down through a lace of elder, thumbs of bracken,
an animal downfall, something stricken
by the weight of winters and history
at the turning of twenty centuries.

Adders

for Christine

That day in June
when the adders hatched,
the hedgers and the ditchers
rumbled the back lanes
in yellow machines.

The main roads done,
shaved to the bone of cow parsley,
stitchwort, Jack-by-the-hedge,
came the turn of the B roads
and numberless lanes.

Young men swung the blades
up and over till the hedge was clipped
close as the hair on their heads
so you'd run your hands over the bristles
and feel them sing.

As they left they came to the door,
told her, 'You'll be all right now',
that they'd smashed with stones
the nest of young adders
asleep in the hedge in a golden knot,

and the mother snake's quicksilver tongue,
the river of her in the grass,
stopped, smashed on the road,
stiffening in the sun,
a shoelace.

Counting Tigers

Wake to a rumbling growl,
your room electric.
Feel your way through the dark.

Unplug the computer, the phone.
Navigate night by the harbour-lights
of video, music centre, fridge.

The freezer purrs,
one green eye open,
but out there night's out of its cage

and you're counting the miles
…one tiger, two tigers, three…
One mile a second, closer,

till sheet metal shakes overhead,
the room's a white stare
and you're scared witless

till the show's over and day dawns,
ordinary, light striping the lawn,
the sun back behind bars.

Breathing

Prowl the house sniffing out gas leaks,
a cloth festering somewhere,
spilt milk, cat-piss, drains.

Such talent needs exercise.
Putting the cat out, inhale her musk
as she pours herself into the night

like your long ago mother, her fur, her Chanel Number 5,
before the whiff of a moonlighting fox,
and frost, and the coats in the hall.

Some smells are faint, the distinct breath
of tap water from each place you have lived,
the twig of witch hazel two rooms away.

Some are stolen like honey, the secretive salts
of skin, in Waterstone's, say, or the bank,
as you lean together, breathing.

Or the new-born that smell like the sea
and the darkness we came from, that gasp
of the drowned in a breaking wave.

Taxidermy

She called it 'saving', tenderly
lifting them, hares, barn owls, badgers,
poisoned, killed on the road.
She'd unpeel the skin,
scoop each body clean of its organs.

She'd rob the vaults of the heart,
the skull's ivory,
the music box of the lungs.
the ribbons of muscle,
the arterial arrangements of blood.

Then she'd fill the emptiness,
rolling the skin into place,
stitching it back over nothing
so you'd never know.
What the eye can't see...

She saved this barn owl, real
but for the gleam in its eye,
white wings aloft so you think of angels,
of souls, of the cold children
and their stolen hearts.

Lost, not blood but that little pulse
that used to beat in her throat,
not the heart but its beat,
not the brain but the dream,
not lungs but the tides of the breath,

and mothers, fathers,
once the delta had emptied itself
it was not death, or knowing it
that most hungered and haunted and hurt.
But the thought of it. Stuffed.

Front Page

It's the photograph that does it.
A man howling for his child.
You can't forget it
despite a let up in the rain,
sunlight on a river,
a flight of geese over an estuary.
It's a rucksack of sorrow
on your shoulder, on your mind.

Try leaving it on the platform
to be defused like a suspect package.
Try leaving it on the train,
personal belongings
they remind you to take.
Try to lose, bin, burn it,
indestructible as the polythene
of flowers in a filthy stairwell.

Maybe just this once
we should forego the minute's silence.
Maybe this time, in supermarket,
street and school and public square,
studio, station, stadium,
standing together, eyes closed,
we should throw back our heads
for a one-minute howl.

On the Train

Cradled though England between flooded fields
rocking, rocking the rails, my head-phones on,
the black box of my Walkman on the table.
Hot tea trembles in its plastic cup.
I'm thinking of you waking in our bed
thinking of me on the train. Too soon to phone.

The radio speaks in the suburbs, in commuter towns,
in cars unloading children at school gates,
is silenced in dark parkways down the line
before locks click and footprints track the frost
and trains slide out of stations in the dawn
dreaming their way towards the blazing bone-ship.

The Vodaphone you are calling
may have been switched off.
Please call later. And calling later,
calling later their phones ring in the rubble
and in the rubble of suburban kitchens
the wolves howl into silent telephones.

I phone. No answer. Where are you now?
The train moves homeward through the morning.
Tonight I'll be home safe, but talk to me, please.
Pick up the phone. Today I'm tolerant
of mobiles. Let them say it. I'll say it too.
Darling, I'm on the train.

A Death in the Village

The lanes are under snow of the thorn
and weighed with chains of wild laburnum
and nothing's different about the day,
except for the 'never again' death speaks.

We stop at the next farm to share the news
with our neighbour. 'A lovely man.'
For a while he's at the heart
of our talk and our silence

when everything shifts a bit –
a widow, a farm, a funeral,
his workshop where at this moment
sunlight is casting a dust-sheet

over oil guns, solder, an old lathe,
the things an engineer keeps, in case,
the secrets of a man and a shed,
its seemly disorder and grace.

Only last week, bringing us tools,
he stepped in to admire the joinery
in our new room, and spoke of a carpenter
he knew, suddenly, shockingly dead.

'You never know', he will always say
when it's summer again and the kite flaunts
above the may-trees and golden chain,
'what is before you.'

Stranger on a Train

Nothing out of the way about the man opposite me,
his father pacing the platform, turning away,
his anxious mother, her pale wave unreturned
as the train pulled out of Carmarthen. Ordinary, thirtyish.
Distressed leather bomber, jeans, the ring in his ear.
A seaman, maybe. A soldier. Nothing odd,
but his glittering straightahead unblinking stare.

He didn't once look at the perfect morning,
water meadows watchful with herons,
the sky in the river as the train gave a small shout
and leaned into the curve, cockle gatherers
small as wading birds far out on the estuary,
the slippery wrestle of waters where
the Tywi pours its heart out to the sea.

Ferryside. Cidweli. The train skittering the shore.
His eyes' black stones stared into the void
over my shoulder. I didn't dare move, change seats.
If he were about to gun down the train
I'd be first to go. I thought about smiling,
mentioning the weather, offering a mint.
At Llanelli the mask split in a terrible smile,

At Swansea he left the train,
left two old people in a small Welsh town
alone in the difficult silence,
left me shaking,
left my eyes seared by two white flares,
like when you've glanced by mistake
at the eclipsing sun.

Someone

At first a whirr of moth-wings far away,
a bud of gorse on blue. Already the day
is hurt by news from the East,
bombers strafing villages
and the hard men talking big.

A mile across the fields, at the blind junction
under Banc y Sidan Du, where the lane
that winds up from the village meets the A road,
the helicopter settles delicately
as an orange-tip on gorse.

Two fire engines. An ambulance. Another.
That acid yellow of police and paramedics.
For hours, all purpose gone from our day,
someone's beautiful machinery's unravelled,
sinew, muscle, bone, from steel,

till someone's lifted like a road-crushed hare
in the yellow claws. The propellor turns.
The helicopter tilts and goes, taking your heart,
turns simply till it finds the thermal
and sifts north to where, like television,

hands are waiting to unload someone,
or someone that was, and someone's story
lays its shadow over histories
that cannot be undone. And there's weeping
on the slope of black silk.

Perfecting the Art

Somewhere
there will be a woman
in a car park
unloading a trolley
of the week's necessities.

There will be a man
pulling off the freeway
into the dusk suburb,
parking his car
under falling maple leaves,
slipping a gun from its glove.

On the other side of the world
there will be young men
stepping from the shower,
girls rinsing salt from their hair,
the surf's glamour still on them
like sand on children's skin.

There will be men
parking a car
in a holiday street,
their hearts fired with dreaming,
their brains mechanical,
ticking.

The Night War Broke

the moon stared at the desert
caught the steel of a gun
the eye of a rat

it looked into rooms
at the wideawake in their beds
at their windows
at the whites of their eyes
at their stained faces

it spreadeagled the sea
struck silver for the jet's shadow
lit the deck of the aircraft carrier
for the harrier's foot

struck dumb the sleepless with their radios
in the cities the villages the back of beyond

looked into the pond the bucket the puddle
at the ewes asleep on their shadows
a fox stepping among them
the shepherd's eye
sweeping the pregnant flock

drew blood from the women
drew cries from the babies cut early from their wombs
'to avoid labour in a city at war'
drew afterpains from the uterus
drew milk to the breast on the third day

and somewhere along the line
scrambled language
between lunatic tongue
and the moonstruck
listening in the dark

Tomatoes

Two brothers and a truck
crossing the Tigris
on the road to Baghdad,
stopped at a checkpoint.

Their cargo is fruit for the city market,
not crated, not cradled against a rough ride.
Just a freight of fruit piled like stones
on the road to war.

Hours earlier, by starlight,
under the drums of the dark,
they'd fixed the sides on the flatbed,
passing each nut and bolt till it's done.

Before dawn, hands that sowed seed
on the plains of Tigris, or Euphrates,
that nurtured seedlings with dung
and slaked them with waters of biblical streams,

hands that cupped the craniums of babies
and stroked scared children to sleep,
hands that will fist the heavens with weeping
before it's done, tenderly took in their palms

the cupola of each ripe fruit,
and picked, and filled
every basket, bucket and barrow,
tipping them into the truck,

a pyramid of fruit
bumping north
on the Baghdad road,
piled like skulls.

Making the Beds for the Dead

Ewe

MARCH 2003

No. No money in it. Just this:
the two of us in the field's corner
at the crowning,

to feel the heat of it,
to be here at the continuum,
birth and baptismal,

as where rivers meet
and join and go their way,
keeping to themselves

for a while, cold, whole,
even as they empty themselves
into the great mouth of the sea.

Wethers

Spring-born, their lives lived
on the one slope, in the one flock.
Summer, they forget their mothers,
forget our hands, learn grass,
grow wild, wander afield on the hill.
Winter, they know us again, grow tame,
calling for hay at the gate.

At two years, or three,
in winter they walk to death,
silent but for the muffled drums
of their slipshod feet on the road.
In the yard Dai Esger quiets
each one with voice and hand,
before the gun.

Each death is a silence.
Quicker done,
one by one,
than the rabbit
in the cat's jaws,
than the long going out
of our bedridden suffering old.

Quicker than the flock
tumbrelled down the motorway,
fleece to fleece in the tiered truck
rocking the road, sipping drips
from oil-slicked rain on the slats,
then blood and blunder
in a strange country.

Sheep and Goats

Samarkand, forty degrees centigrade,
sheep tethered in the dust, and men
squatting on carpets in the sand
played cards in a flaunt of hookah smoke,

while in the cool of an interior
a woman milked a goat, her head bowed
over the bowl, as Marged long ago,
listened to the heart-beat of the cow,
fluting milk-notes into a tin bucket.

*

Crete, the week of Easter,
we came down from the mountains to the sea
on the dusty road in the evening,
and saw a man in the courtyard of his house
butchering a goat, spreadeagled in a tree
like a crucifixion.

Flight

DECEMBER 2000

Behind them, the terminal's a mirage
seen through the migraine of heat,
the transitional moment between cooled spaces
a wobbling forty degrees centigrade.
Then seat belt, jet-roar, lift-off,
and gravity grips like body armour
until they are weightless as birds.

Innocently, insolently, almost,
they settle for the journey north
over the oceans, the clouds, the continents,
bearing the perilous seed
packed in its polythene casket
for brothers in a cold city.
Sweetmeats. Spices. Raw meat.

Silks for sisters. Language
to warm a mother's exile.
Traditional clothes for nieces and nephews
who pretend to be glad
but would rather have Levis,
strange meats the young ones taste
and bin, the cooked with the raw.

★

A northern city celebrates
the holy feasts of winter, its streets
gaudy with gold. In back alleys
behind restaurants, stray dogs and tramps
plunder the bins for bones,
scraps, scrapings, festering waste,
where the virus breeds in secret.
The rest awaits the pig-swill man at dawn.

Virus

You have to admire its beauty,
its will to live,
fizzing in a soup of chemicals,
wanting nothing but a living host
to practise symmetry
and cell division.

Brought from space
on the heel of a star,
a primitive chemical
seething in soupy pools,
its arithmetic heart
bent on sub-division, multiplication.

On screen, an image
of rotational symmetry
in a box of glass,
a spaceman tumbling
in a two-fold turn,
weightless in his hurtling ship.

Or still life,
computer generated,
a dandelion head, each seed a field,
folding, unfolding flower
smaller than a bacterium,
butting blind towards the living cell.

So where did it start?
Somewhere hot and far away
where they don't fill in forms
to take a sheep to market,
don't call a beast a product,
a commodity.

Where they kill a lamb with a knife at its throat,
and God who loves the lilies of the field
and the one lamb which is lost,
forgot this one with her little,
clicking, cloven, high-heeled hooves,
the horizon in her golden eye.

Silence

FEBRUARY 2001

First the animals lost their voices,
then the people.
'We couldn't speak.
We could only hold each other.'

Words drowned in a howl of wind,
in the howl of a man in a hollow barn.
Syllables shredded like wool on the wire,
dissolved in a rap of rain.

Language lost in the squalor,
squealing swine sickening
in the filthy sheds
at Heddon-on-the Wall,

bedded in hogwash,
fed on raw leavings,
crusts, rinds, peelings,
putrefying meat.

Lost in the mountain talk
of ewe and lamb,
in the moan of cattle in milk,
in the call at the door

of strangers dressed to kill,
in the whine of a dog
in the empty yard.
in the words on the weasel's tongue.

*

'We couldn't swallow or speak.
So quiet it was unnatural.
Not even the birds were singing.
Silence you could feel, cold on you,
like snow.'

Carlisle
FEBRUARY 2001

This little piggy went to market,
This little piggy stayed home.
This little piggy was fed raw meat.
This little piggy had none.
This little piggy wheezed into the wind,
and the virus flew all the way home.

On the Move
FEBRUARY 2001

From Heddon-on-the-Wall,
Foot and Mouth.
Traed a Genau.
Too far away to worry.

But it travels like loose talk,
on the tongue, on the hoof,
on the air, word of mouth,
faster than breathing.

Market to motorway,
trucked from the north
to an Essex slaughterhouse,
bought cheap, sold dear.

On wheels, on foot,
on the breath, on the wind
in the slipstream of trucks,
the meat dealers banking the profits.

'I sold my sheep in Shrewsbury market.
I had no idea they travelled so far.'

No Entry
MARCH 2001

It's over the border, across the bridge.
In Ceredigion, public footpaths
are closed for fear of it.

Kids step off the school bus in the lane
and go straight home. Cooped up, captive,
they play indoors, alone, on line.

Farms look narrow-eyed up stony tracks,
squinting through curtains of long grass
across barricades of disinfected straw.

First Lamb
12TH MARCH 2001

Brand new and steaming
in the morning sun, the ewe
in an ecstacy of instinct.

For a moment we forget
the lorries and the fires,
the hooded men, the smell,

and think, 'In years to come
she'll still be with us, the long line
of her descendants grazing the hill.'

Lamb on a Mobile Phone
MARCH 2001

Lamb number ten,
born in the silence of a cold blue night
under the flightpath of kite and satellite
four hundred miles away.

And born here too, tonight,
in the rumpus of the city,
where meat comes wrapped and bloodless
in its polystyrene tray,

and the cry of a lamb
in a city restaurant
from your mobile phone to mine
is a sound clean as a star,

a string of syllables
whose sound-waves lap
at the pavements of the city
and the way we live.

Born under stars as numerous
as spores of the virus, as atoms of bone,
as particles of blood on the wind
when the gun is fired.

Rumour

Wool on the wire.
Wind in the gate.
Traed a genau.
Foot and mouth.
The virus on the move
like whispers.

The builder saying:
'There are people
getting rich on this',
as he scrubs,
and changes his boots in the van.

Every farm fortified
by a prickly thicket
of straw at the gate,
buckets and a brush
to dip your boots,
to wash your wheels,
to scour your soul.

The word's on the run,
on the phone.
An anonymous stranger
to a friend of a friend
tried again trading
traed a genau
in a layby on the M4.

For the compensation,
to get out now
while the going's bad.
Say the whispers,
say signs on the gate
traed a genau.

Plague
SPRING 2001

On television, corpses are piled on carts.
on distant farms with strangers at their gates.

Stiff-legged as chairs, the animals burn,
old furniture on a bonfire, not flesh and bone,

thrown upside-down and awkward to the flames.
A pedigree Holstein with a fancy name

hangs, grotesque from the JCB hook
against an inferno of flame and smoke.

★

It's closer by the day,
its secret footprints

on the ground we walk on,
on the wheels of our cars,

on paw and wing,
on the breath of beasts, on the wind.

And every day the cities, suburbs, towns,
seem further off, their distance greatening.

★

The man on the timber lorry from Shropshire
won't step down. He blows the horn,
hands each plank to us and drives away
having never set foot in Ceredigion.

We put a bin by the gate for the post,
a boot-brush and buckets of kill-germ
for washing the dust and the plague
from travellers' feet at our door.

★

'Why can't we vaccinate?
It's no worse than 'flu.
They'll be shooting people next.'

★

'It's the market.
It's the ministry.
It's the NFU.
It's the government.'

Marsh Fritillary

This could get out of hand,
shake settled things,
rival the good life and the way things are,
shifting the very ground
beneath our feet.

Take Devil's Bit Scabious and the Marsh Fritillary,
interdependent and inseparable
in perfect balance, a flower, a butterfly
among the scabious on Cors Llawr Cwrt,
in the richest colony in Europe.

Each quivering insect turning on its toes
is the double mirror of itself,
in the melt-water of glaciers, where time has spent
an ice age and what followed making right
a scrape of land for a flower and a butterfly.

Hywel's Story

'The '60s. I was out with the gun after rabbits, or a fox.
I walked to the end of the wood, real quiet. I looked over the fence
at that secret field between the two woods. I was looking for mushrooms.
Something wrong with those cattle. They were lying down, standing,
any old how, alone facing the fence, heads down, not grazing.
Not together all one way like when it's going to rain.

A lazy farmer. Always in the pub. Neglected his animals.
No talk of traed a genau then, but the word went round.
His cows got over it and no harm done. Makes you think.'

Family
JUNE 2001

They stand at the gate
so still and silent
they could be a portrait,
undated, anywhere,
endurance bred into them
like the heft in the flock.

The camera holds them,
red-eyed against hills and sky.
Over their shoulders a golden emptiness
where every summer of their lives
hay was cut, or silage,
children tossing hay in the sun.

They'll clean up and start again,
but they'll never hear the wind
sing in the pipes of the gate,
the whine and bump of silage machines
for the depth charge of flame
then the outroar of burning.

And the smell. Never again will a field
breathe grass-saps and pollens
and the sigh of a shower
drying in the heat of the day,
for the stench of putrefaction,
burning tar, burning flesh.

Cull

SUMMER 2001

They bring them from the hills
as they've always done,
shepherd and dog, a whistle
in the air like an arrow,
the flock a waterfall
gleaming on a dusk hill.

Below is the black dark
where sheep are a kind of silence
that knows the mountain
by the heft of stone and sky,
and a lit window is lonelier
than no window at all.

At Storey Arms tonight
that lay-by under Pen-y-fan
where we used to stop with the children
is a theatre of death.
The slaughtermen work
into the night by floodlamps.

There are lorries on the pass,
the smell of blood,
and fire in the sky where once
so long ago I don't know if it's true,
my father and I watched a car in flames
on the mountain and a man running,

and he's still running,
haunting the pass between one thing and another,
one day smoke in a chimney,
next, the wall gives, like the bitch
in my arms when the vet came,
or the lamb you brought from the snow.

When it's done
the hills will be dark again,
not a light left burning.
Just the weather
waiting in the wings
to finish the job.

Pigs

SUMMER 2001

Confrontation on an organic pig-farm.
The farmer faces out the ministry men
dressed to kill, reasonable, just doing their job.
A decent man, the farmer loves his beasts,
refuses to call home the suckling sows,
refuses to lure the easy creatures
with the voice they know, buckets of meal.

Wallowing in the sun, the great sows doze,
their healthy nakedness in the open air
a flaunt, an afront to men from the ministry.
He will not call them trotting on delicate toes
home, each to its ark, to be killed.
'Collateral' they call it. The word is out,
a neighbour's infected cattle for the cull.

Woolmark

'A hobby flock', said the ministry,
'must be sacrified for the common good.'

She wouldn't be moved,
rounding her little flock
into her front room like snowdrifts
muffling the three piece and the piano,
shut the door on wall-to-wall fleece
and to hell with the mess.

You couldn't blame her.
I'd have hidden mine too.
Whatever it cost, thumb in the dyke
against the force of the rising flood
till they came to arrest her, driving
her ewes and new lambs to their death.

★

A man in a field with a rifle,
firing at sheep, hit and miss.
'It shouldn't have happened,'
they said. 'We will look into it.'

The Vet

'I worked from six in the morning until gone midnight. One night I slept in my truck.
I'm used to death. I had to put down eighty baby lambs by humane injection.
I couldn't talk about it for a month or so.'

Number eighty's going nowhere,
hot, alive and up on trembling legs,
an hour old, still damp and yolky,

She smells of the sea, the umbilical
a wet tendril against his hand,
her hooves wave-washed pebbles.

He's been up all night committing
the new-born to death, four to a sack.
He's had enough. A grown man weeping.

The last lamb's quiet for the needle,
her body quivering warm against his chest.
Her ears are leaves between his fingers.

★

It was like this many times over,
grief for the many and the few,
for the special one, the farm-child's pet,
the *swci* they raised on the bottle,
the beast that took first at the show,
the flock locked in a farm kitchen,
the house cow, the goat on a ribbon.

None spared by the ministry men,
the vets, the slaughtermen.
The sick, the healthy,
the rag-tag, the beautiful,

stood for the gun, one by one.
Some shuddered as they fell.
Some stood still, surprised,
and folded in a river of blood.

Night after night
we watched them die,
beasts thrown to the flames
like sinners consumed.

Fox

SEPTEMBER 2001

First foot in the night fields
down river, across border,
after feasting with crows
on the carcass of a sheep.

Little cat-dog gorged on flesh.
What she can't eat she stashes
in her dozen larders
against hard times.

On the farm track she laps rain
from a cloven pool,
leaving cells to multiply
in the soup of a hoof print.

Sunrise, and the cattle
come home for milking,
slowly, heavily picking their way,
rolling their oiled machinery,

all angles and corners,
old leather toolbags
of hammers and saws,
shoulders and shanks.

On the track they pause
in the footfall of the sun
for a snatch of grass,
a sip from the chalice.

September 2001

before the 11th day

'They didn't punish the people.
They punished the animals.'

★

'It's Biblical. Like a terrible warning.'

★

after the 11th day

'How could we know there was worse to come?
The world has changed forever.'

★

'Before this your life was your own.
You could plan for the future.'

★

'I didn't know there were people walking this earth
who would burn human beings like cattle.'

★

'All year I've been obsessed with the virus.
September, and the end in sight.
Then this. Life will never be the same again.'

★

'It's not just us weeping now,
but everyone weeping
and the world black as sin.'

The Fall

We watched them fall
like leaves, rubble, dust,
limbs akimbo on the air

as if arms could be wings,
as if men and women could be angels
as if birds gliding the thermals of blast
mirrored and broken in waterfalling walls
might spread their wings
slow their fall
lend them flight
as if God would extend a hand
and set them down on the pavement
into safe hands

too far to hear their screams,
or the screech of accelerating air
bandage their mouths
stuffing our throats with ashes
filling the lungs of the falling
of the fallen
of the fleeing
of those following the news
with the particulates, poisons,
fumes, false gods, fanaticisms of terror.

Now they are myth,
archaeology, geology.
They have turned to stone,
the murdered and the murderers.
They have become the city,
igneous, sedimentary,
pressed between strata
of steel, glass, concrete,
time compressed in a moment
in the long making of stone.

The slow evolution of the world is over,
and never, never again
will retina or memory or soul be free
of our second fall from grace,
or be washed clean of that stain.

Three Minutes

The brightest morning,
the darkest day,
as every habitation on the earth
fills up with ashes
blown by an old wind.

Along silk-road, sea-lane, flight-path,
by radio wave and winking satellite,
comes news of the ruined city,
and every human hand
holds a bowl of dust.

In my daughter's house
– her new house, still filled
with the crated rubble of the old one –
we unwrap crockery,
undressing piece by piece
from crumpled newspapers
blurred with words from before we knew
that a cup could be a chalice of blood.

At the stroke of the hour
as Europe falls silent
we stand three minutes
in the world's company,
before, like everywhere, we turn
wordless to the ordinary,
unwrapping, washing, drying, stowing
one cup of gall at a time.

Shepherd
DECEMBER

Christmas, and over the snow
a jet chases the day,
cresting the sill of the land
to take the Atlantic.

In the fields
a man and his dog
check the sheep dawn and dusk
as they've always done.

What's it to him,
the flight of kings,
but to remind him
that the world turns,

that going home is a prayer,
that even war draws breath.

Blackface

MARCH 2002

So it's come to this.
Just a sheep. Blackface.
'Never name them,' they warned.
One of our first eight,
seven Beulah specklefaced,
and this one, odd one out,
bold, vocal, always first to the gate
foraging our hands for gifts.

Ten years on, too old for the ram,
we kept her, the favourite.
Then, that October ram-raid, the broken gate.
A gang of males penned a year too long
by Livestock Movement Restrictions,
by protecting the market,
by money, dealer-men, meat.

Two nights and a second dawn,
and we're on our knees in the straw,
her head on my arm,
my fingers deep in her wool
till the pulse in her neck
fades to a flutter
guttering out in the dark.

We dig in the rain and wind,
topsoil, shale, a layer of clay,
red earth, the field's geology.
The deepest grave we've ever had to dig.
We line it with hay then turn to carry her,
swollen and slippery, stiffening already,
so heavy I'm scared we'll stumble.

We lower what's left of her,
like the millions they threw on the pyres
in the days of the virus.
What gets us is that tender glimpse
like a sanctuary lamp
at the door of the vulva,
and the lamb dead in the boat of her body.

There's a pen to be cleaned,
fresh straw to be laid. Hay. Water.
I bring in a new one, a ewe and her lamb,
for checking, safe from fox and weather,
the pretty one with the white face
scattered with freckles,
like a flower. Flowerface. Maybe.

On Banc Blaen Cwrt

2003

The sheep are huddled,
hurdled in the *lloc*,
in the shade of a larch wood.
The hottest summer in memory
and the flock's overdressed,
woolsacks waiting
for the evening shearers,

To the wrist in her fleece,
he checks her for footrot, blowfly,
kneels to the task, speaking low
to each ewe turned over, helpless
in the chair of his thighs,
till she groans to her feet
and steps away tenderly.

The dog quivers with the thrill of it,
nose under the gate.
Not naming but knowing each one,
he counts them out,
twenty and their lambs,
cirrus cloud gathering.
to wait for the drama,

men setting stage
with wires and extensions,
woolsacks agape for the sweet
lanolin smell of warm fleece,
a platform laid down on the grass
for the tapdance of hooves on wood,
to the humdrum buzzing of shears.

Birthday

As midnight moved through the time zones
the comet travelled, farther and farther
from the earth's memory.
The last light swept the sea,

over Land's End, Finisterre,
before the black Atlantic and the stars.
Between them a ship gleamed,
a Boeing blinked in the dark.

The world up late, and for a moment
we were nowhere, tuning our broken instruments
to the winds of Mars. Midnight touched the clocks,
the whole world torched by the moment,

but for the silent in the besieged city,
their mouths the O's of sorrow crying zero
into the black mouths of guns. Will pity
save them? It'll take a miracle.

Aftermath

The moon stares at the desert,
the dust and the detritus,
the nuzzling warhead,

at the earth's shudder,
dust settling
on a shaken world,

lights the road for the lost,
the footloose, the fugitive,
the warriors and the wounded,

lays linen on the fields,
on beasts asleep on their shadows
in the silver breath of the night,

looks into wind-crumpled water
at the cold bone of its face,
strikes gold in a pond

where the otter has left
two prints, and the peeled skull
of a frog, like the husk of a planet.

Flood

When all's said
and done
if civilisation drowns
the last colour to go
will be gold –
the light on a glass,
the prow of a gondola,
the name on a rosewood piano
as silence engulfs it,

and first to return
to a waterlogged world,
the rivers slipping out to sea,
the cities steaming,
will be gold,
one dip from Bellini's brush,
feathers of angels,
Cinquecento nativities,
and all that follows.